AF270593

# THE UNABOMBER

## BY TOM STREISSGUTH

AMERICAN
CRIME
STORIES

Essential Library

An Imprint of Abdo Publishing | abdobooks.com

**ABDOBOOKS.COM**

Published by Abdo Publishing, a division of ABDO, PO Box 398166, Minneapolis, Minnesota 55439. Copyright © 2024 by Abdo Consulting Group, Inc. International copyrights reserved in all countries. No part of this book may be reproduced in any form without written permission from the publisher. Essential Library™ is a trademark and logo of Abdo Publishing.

Printed in the United States of America, North Mankato, Minnesota.
102023
012024

Cover Photo: John Youngbear/AP Images
Interior Photos: Charles Knoblock/AP Images, 5; Dale Gerhard/The Press of Atlantic City/AP Images, 10; Evergreen High School Yearbook/AP Images, 13, 15; Liz Albro Photography/Shutterstock Images, 19; Scott Manchester/Sygma/Getty Images, 21; Rich Pedrocelli/AFP/Getty Images, 23, 90–91; Shutterstock Images, 24; Elaine Thompson/AP Images, 26; FBI, 29, 49; Bettmann/Getty Images, 33; Ken Wolter/Shutterstock Images, 35; Bob Black/Chicago Sun-Times/AP Images, 38–39; Michael Macor/The San Francisco Chronicle/Hearst Newspapers/Getty Images, 43, 45, 55, 75; Sean Pavone/Shutterstock Images, 46; E. Jason Wambsgans/Chicago Tribune/Tribune News Service/Getty Images, 52; John G. Mabanglo/AFP/Getty Images, 58; James Keyser/The Chronicle Collection/Getty Images, 60; Steven Lewis/AP Images, 61; Rich Pedroncelli/AP Images, 65, 77; Doug Mills/AP Images, 67; Evan Agostini/Hulton Archive/Getty Images, 68, 80; David Goldman/AP Images, 71; Red Line Editorial, 73; Michael Macor/The San Francisco Chronicle/AP Images, 85; KPIX-TV San Francisco/AP Images, 88

Editor: Arnold Ringstad
Series Designer: Melissa Martin

Library of Congress Control Number: 2023939445



**PUBLISHER'S CATALOGING-IN-PUBLICATION DATA**

Names: Streissguth, Tom, author.
Title: The Unabomber / by Tom Streissguth
Description: Minneapolis, Minnesota: Abdo Publishing, 2024 | Series: American crime stories | Includes online resources and index.
Identifiers: ISBN 9781098292157 (lib. bdg.) | ISBN 9798384910091 (ebook)
Subjects: LCSH: Crime and criminals--Juvenile literature. | Killing (Murder)--Juvenile literature. | United States--Juvenile literature. | Kaczynski, Theodore John, 1942--Juvenile literature. | Unabomber, 1942--Juvenile literature. | Terrorist bombings--Juvenile literature. | Serial murderers--Juvenile literature.
Classification: DDC 364.97--dc23

# CONTENTS

This book discusses accounts of crime, violence, and death that may be disturbing to some readers.

# JUST ANOTHER DAY

The package lay on the ground, abandoned near a car in the middle of a parking lot. It appeared to be a paper bag, though there was nothing on the bag showing what might be inside. The date was May 25, 1978, and the place was the Chicago Circle campus of the University of Illinois.

Mary Gutierrez walked across the lot. She spotted the bag and went over to inspect it. Inside was a wrapped package covered in ten uncanceled $1 stamps featuring American playwright Eugene O'Neill. The parcel was ready for mailing. It was addressed to a Professor E. J. Smith of the School of Engineering at Rensselaer Polytechnic Institute in Troy, New York. It also had a return address listing Buckley Crist Jr. of the Northwestern University Technological Institute in Evanston, Illinois.

**The Chicago Circle campus of the University of Illinois was the site where the Unabomber's first bomb was discovered, beginning a string of bombings that would continue for 17 years.**

Evanston was not far, only about a 40-minute drive away. Had Crist himself been here? Had he somehow forgotten this package or perhaps dropped it? It seemed an unlikely thing to do. If the parcel was carefully addressed and stamps were put on it, why leave it in an empty lot where it was bound to be stolen or thrown away? Gutierrez took it home and contacted Crist, who sent someone to retrieve the parcel.

When the package arrived at his office at Northwestern, the professor had a long look at it. He had never seen it before, and he had no idea what it was. He did not know who might have put his name on it. Instead of opening it, he called the campus police.

## The First Victim

Officer Terry Marker of Northwestern campus security responded to Crist's call about a suspicious parcel sent from Chicago. Arriving at Crist's office, Marker wasn't sure what to make of the package. He began opening it.

Marker didn't realize the mysterious parcel contained a long wooden box enclosing a nine-inch (23 cm) length of galvanized iron pipe. The pipe was sealed at both ends. Inside it were two different kinds of smokeless powder as well as match heads. A nail was held in place with heavy rubber bands, ready to strike the match heads. A small door was cut into one of the short ends of the box. The word "Open" was written in Sharpie pen, with a small arrow pointing to the door.

Marker opened the door. The rubber band snapped, and the nail struck the match heads. The match heads ignited, setting off the powder inside the pipe. The box exploded, burning and cutting Marker's hands. With this blast, the terrorist who came to be known as the Unabomber had injured the first of his many victims.

**In all, the Unabomber carried out 16 bombing attacks.[1] His devices either failed to work or were defused in only two of those cases.**

# The Investigation

Sixteen years later, the Federal Bureau of Investigation (FBI) was still working to unravel the mysteries of the explosive parcel found in a parking lot in 1978. Since then, a person or group had been mailing or leaving bombs meant to kill or maim victims selected seemingly at random. More than a dozen people had been injured or killed. The attack at the University of Illinois was only the first.

The FBI had been working on the case since 1979. The agency used a six-letter acronym to identify the investigation: UNABOM, which stood for "university and airlines bomber." Some of the early attacks had been targeted at university and airline personnel. The suspect became known as the Unabomber. The FBI had put hundreds of agents and lab workers on the case.

Bomb and forensics experts studied the explosion sites, while a profiler worked up a personality profile for the Unabomber. But there was little evidence to go on. FBI agent Kathleen Puckett explained, "The profiling unit usually has a lot of evidence at a scene to review to come up with

## THE LONGEST CASE

The investigation of the Unabomber was one of the longest and most expensive in FBI history. By the time the case was solved, the agency had employed more than 150 agents to track down the killer.[2] The case ran from 1979 to 1996, but it wasn't the longest-running investigation in FBI history. That distinction belongs to the investigation of an airline hijacking that took place in 1971. A man who came to be known as D. B. Cooper boarded a flight, demanded a ransom and a parachute, and then jumped out of the plane over Washington State. Cooper was never identified or apprehended.

a profile of an unknown offender. In this case, they had no latent fingerprints, no hair and fibers that led anywhere. . . . some of these devices along the way, the batteries were even stripped. You couldn't even trace the batteries back to where they were purchased or acquired."[3]

Despite a significant investment of time and effort, along with a million-dollar reward offered to the public for information, the FBI still didn't even have a suspect sixteen years later, much less an arrest. Nor had the bureau been able to answer a simple question about the Unabomber's very first bomb. Why go to the trouble of preparing a package to be mailed, with a return address and $10 worth of stamps, only to leave it on the ground?

Three FBI agents had thought of a possible answer and decided to test their theory. They determined the dimensions of the explosive parcel. Then they searched through postal

## A DOUBLE IDENTITY?

For a time, some believed that the Unabomber may have been the same person as the Zodiac killer. This serial killer was active in California in the 1960s and early 1970s, and investigators eventually learned that the perpetrator behind the bombings lived in the state around the same time. The Zodiac killer selected and shot his victims seemingly at random, and he sent taunting letters and coded messages to newspapers. However, the FBI eventually ruled out this possibility, in part because the Unabomber exclusively used bombs, not guns, in his crimes. The Zodiac killer has never been caught.

The FBI's James Fitzgerald was among the many agents who worked the Unabomber case over its long history.

records to figure out what size mailbox was nearby in 1978. With this information at hand, the investigators concluded they had been right—the box would not have fit into the mailbox. The bomber had simply abandoned the package on the ground.

To the agents, this discovery, along with other clues about the early bombings, suggested that the bomber was familiar with the Chicago area. He may have even lived there at the time of the initial attacks. By continuing to build a profile of their infamous suspect, the FBI was closer than ever before to figuring out the identity of the Unabomber.

In the early 1990s, the FBI created a document to collect all of its findings about the Unabomber case in one place. It was called "UNABOM Known Facts, Fiction, and Theory."

# CHAPTER TWO

# DROPPING OUT

Theodore "Ted" Kaczynski was born on May 22, 1942, in Chicago. His parents were Theodore, who went by "Turk," and Wanda Kaczynski. When Ted was ten years old, the family moved from Chicago to Evergreen Park, just west of the city. They lived in a small, neat suburban house as Ted and his younger brother, David, grew up and attended local public schools.

Ted was a smart and capable student. He showed an aptitude for mathematics, but he had some problems with his math teachers, whom he would sometimes correct in class. When he was in fifth grade, his school gave him an intelligence test that suggested he had a genius-level IQ. After this result, the school allowed Ted to skip sixth grade and go straight to junior high.

At home, Ted's father converted an attic space into a bedroom for his elder son. Like Turk, Ted was good with his

**Ted, *bottom*, was pictured alongside fellow scholarship finalists in his high school yearbook.**

hands and skilled at designing and building small machines and woodworking projects. Once the attic bedroom was finished, Ted moved in and set up a workspace. He spent many hours by himself in this room, reading and working on various contraptions.

Ted's brother, David, was seven years younger. David wasn't as academically gifted as his brother, but he seemed to have more friends than Ted. When David asked his mom about this, she replied that Ted was a special kid. He was good at math and other subjects at school, but he liked to spend much of his time alone.

In his mom's opinion, David didn't need to worry about these differences. Wanda told him there was plenty of room in the world for different kinds of people. "Ted . . . was special because he was so intelligent," David explained in *Every Last Tie,* a book he later wrote about his brother. "In the Kaczynski family, intelligence carried high value."[1]

## A Bit of a Loner

In high school, Ted skipped another grade, this time junior year. When he started his senior year, he was just 15 years old. This made him a bit of an outcast. Some of the seniors were hostile and looked down on him. They saw him as an overachieving geek. The fact that Ted often carried his books and papers around in a briefcase didn't help.

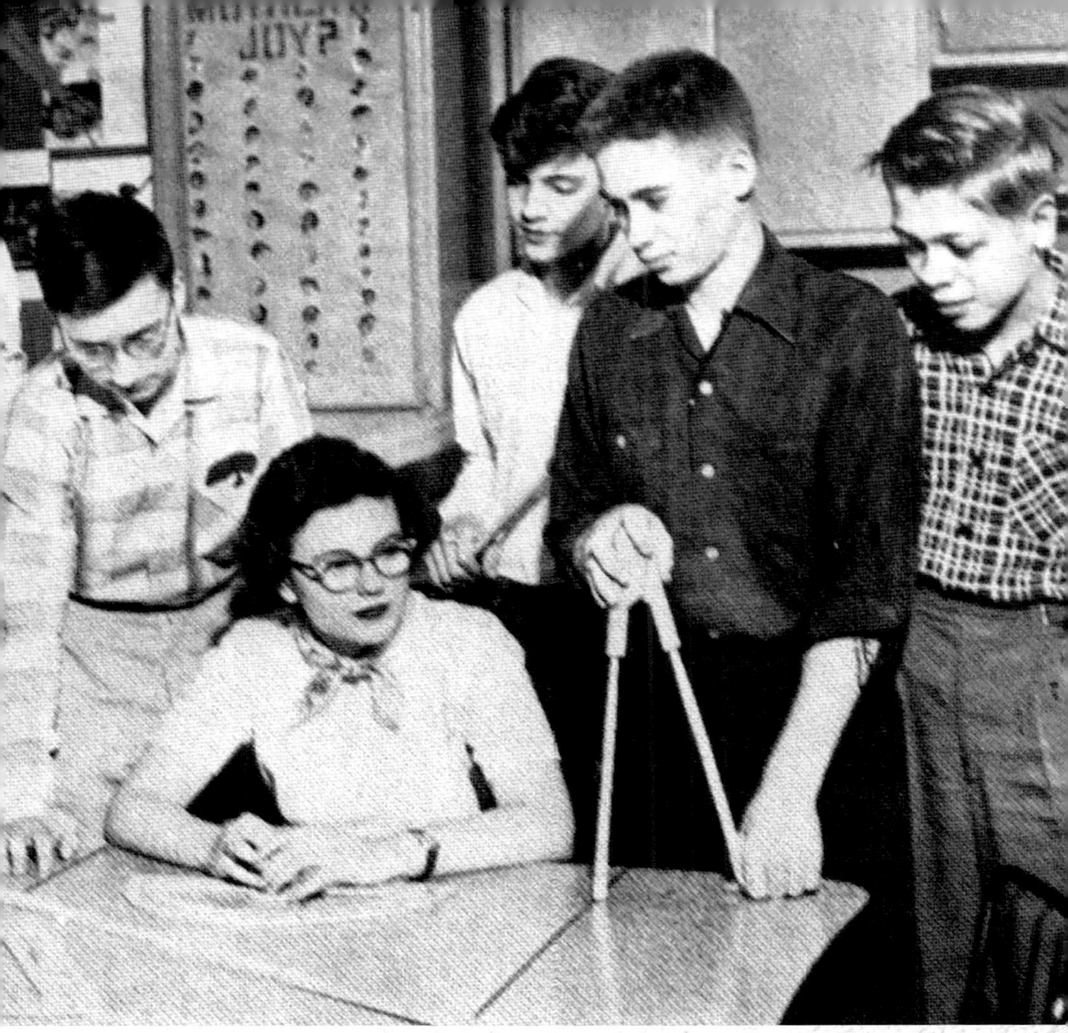

Ted, *third from right*, appeared in a math team group photo
in his school's 1958 yearbook.

That didn't stop Ted from joining several school clubs,
including the chess, biology, German, and math clubs. He was a
dedicated reader and spent many of his free hours with books
of history, philosophy, math, and science. Ted also had a knack
for music. He played the trombone, and he wrote original
pieces for a family trio. His brother was on trumpet, and his
father played piano.

Turk was proud of his son and always pushed him to achieve more. He agreed with the school's idea to let Ted skip his junior year, although some friends of the family advised against it. They thought he wasn't mature enough for the senior class. But in Turk's eyes, Ted's academic achievements were a badge of honor. They reflected well on how the family had raised him.

Ted graduated from high school at age 16. He had been accepted at Harvard University, one of the toughest and most well-regarded universities in the country. To his teachers and his family, he seemed to have a brilliant future.

## Life at Harvard

For his first year at college, Ted lived in a house set aside for younger freshmen. He lived alone in a small single room, where he studied mathematics as well as required general education courses. He joined the swimming and wrestling teams, and for a brief time he also played trombone in the Harvard band.

In his sophomore year, Ted volunteered to be a subject in a psychology experiment. Along with about 20 other Harvard students, he was asked to fill out a questionnaire and write essays describing his outlook on life, his personal religious and political beliefs, and his views on society at large. The study was led by Henry Murray, director of the Harvard Psychological Clinic.

After turning in their essays and questionnaires, the subjects were asked to sit in a room with electrodes attached to their bodies to measure heart rate, blood pressure, and other physical functions. They were then joined by graduate students working for Murray. The graduate students spent

## HENRY MURRAY

Henry Murray was a leading American psychologist of the 1900s. His academic background was in medicine and biochemistry. He switched to psychology after reading the works of Carl Jung, a Swiss thinker who believed humans were affected by ancient, ingrained myths and archetypes. During World War II (1939–1945), the US government asked Murray to work up a detailed psychological study of the German dictator Adolf Hitler.

In the 1930s, Murray had developed the Thematic Apperception Test (TAT). The TAT consists of a series of pictures that the subject is asked to describe. The TAT was used to screen applicants to Harvard in Kaczynski's time, and many psychologists still use the TAT to evaluate and diagnose their patients.

hours criticizing the essays while belittling and insulting the subjects. Murray's goal was to measure the physical stress these confrontations caused to the subjects.

## Moving Up

As a Harvard upperclassman, Ted moved in to Eliot House. This was one of Harvard's big residential houses and one of the oldest, built in 1931. He again lived in a single room, part of a suite on an upper floor that housed five other students. His suitemates saw him only as he rushed in and out of his room, usually slamming the door behind him.

Like the other houses, Eliot had its own wood-paneled dining hall. Here Ted would usually sit by himself, avoiding conversation. When his suitemates would come to his table, he would sometimes just get up and leave. Although they didn't see him or talk to him much, his suitemates sometimes heard him late at night. He would practice the trombone, bumping his chair against the wall of the room while he played.

## Professor of Mathematics

Ted Kaczynski graduated from Harvard in 1962 with a degree in mathematics. In the same year, he enrolled at the University of Michigan and continued his studies in math. There he wrote a PhD thesis on the theme of boundary functions. This was an area of mathematics that few people outside of university-level

Eliot House, featuring a signature green dome, is still a residential house at Harvard today.

math departments understood or knew anything about. But his thesis was accepted, and in 1967 the university awarded him a doctorate.

That fall, Kaczynski accepted a position as an assistant professor of mathematics at the University of California, Berkeley. But by the time he began teaching at Berkeley, he was holding a secret that he wouldn't admit until much later. He had no intention, by this time, of leading the safe and ordinary life of a university math professor. His goal was to save enough money to drop out of society entirely and live off the land in some remote stretch of forest or isolated mountainside.

Ted Kaczynski was building up a powerful contempt for mainstream America. He felt a hatred for politicians, the media, and modern industry. He saw technology and science as evils that were destroying the human spirit. He had his own role in this system as a teacher of mathematics. In a letter

**When the University of California, Berkeley, hired Ted Kaczynski as an associate professor, he was just 25 years old. At the time, he was the youngest professor the university had ever hired.**

to his parents, he explained his resignation after two years of teaching as a way of protesting technology's threat to human freedom. By the time he left Berkeley, these ideas were leading to another goal: violent revenge against the modern world.

Kaczynski resigned from his position at Berkeley just two years after starting there.

# CHAPTER THREE

# SEARCHING FOR WILDERNESS

Like his brother, David Kaczynski felt alienated from modern society. David sought a higher calling, a sense of purpose, and personal fulfillment. For a time, the Kaczynski brothers also shared an ambition to live independently. They each dreamed of seeking out solitude in some untouched stretch of mountain or desert and living off the land, removing themselves from the problems of the modern world.

David graduated from Columbia University in 1970. Ted joined him in a search for their private wilderness. The brothers traveled to Canada, where empty land in the vast country was plentiful and cheap. They found a parcel that looked promising in British Columbia, a western province. The Kaczynskis filed an application for a homesteading permit with the government

**David Kaczynski felt similarly to Ted in the early 1970s, but the brothers' paths soon diverged.**

of Canada. This would allow them to buy the land and build a structure on it.

While waiting for a response, Ted moved back home to Evergreen Park to live with Wanda and Turk. David moved out to Great Falls, Montana. He took a job with the Anaconda Company at the big mining company's zinc smelter in Black Eagle. This town lay just across the Missouri River from Great Falls.

## A Fateful Visit

Montana attracted David just as it drew many other young nature-seekers. It was a big state with plenty of wide-open

The area around Great Falls, Montana, is known for its vast wilderness and sparse population, making it ideal for those seeking isolation.

spaces and inexpensive land. The Rocky Mountains rose in the western half of the state, from Yellowstone National Park in the south to Glacier National Park on the Canadian border. There were grazing lands for cattle ranchers and promising hillsides for gold and silver prospectors.

In the spring of 1971, Ted came to Montana to visit his brother. The Canadian government had denied their application to buy land, so they began looking for another property. Searching the listings at real estate offices, they came across a parcel of 1.4 acres (0.6 ha) on a hillside near the small town of Lincoln, about 90 miles (145 km) from Great Falls. The land was being offered by logger Cliff Gehring, who was selling off a portion of his property to raise money. In June 1971, the Kaczynski brothers bought the land for $2,100, splitting the cost fifty-fifty between them.[1]

David did not move to the property. But soon after they bought the land, Ted began raising a simple cabin there that was 10 feet (3 m) wide and 14 feet (4.3 m) long. Built from scrap lumber Ted scrounged at local yards and sawmills, the structure had just a single room. Ted put in a small vegetable garden and a root cellar to hold his produce through the long winters. For washing and cooking, he collected water from an adjoining creek.

Ted prepared to settle into his new home. By this time, he had resolved to set himself apart from the mainstream.

Ted's small cabin in the woods was simplistic,
with no running water or electric service.

By living on this patch of land, he would prove he had no need
for science, technology, or so-called progress. He also wanted
to push his own family and the academic world into the past.
He wrote letters to his brother, penned essays, and kept a diary.
Ted also tried to come up with a way to fight back against the
modern world.

One of his essays ran 23 pages. It talked about the need
to form an organization that would fight scientific research.

Ted believed that it was
wrong for corporations
and the government
to spend money on
this research. He also
believed that David was
the right person to head
the organization.

Ted sent the essay to
David in a letter. Although
he had no interest in
helping create an antiresearch organization, David kept the
essay, along with many of the letters Ted had written to him,
in the Kaczynski house in Evergreen Park. David recognized
his elder brother as intelligent, and he believed these writings
might someday hold some value for the world.

## FILLING PAGES

Kaczynski was a tireless writer. He kept a
long-running journal of his thoughts and
ideas. After his capture and sentencing,
he corresponded with many people who
wrote to him from outside the prison
walls. He donated his manuscripts, along
with the many letters he received, to the
University of Michigan Library. These
papers fill more than 90 boxes in the
library's collections.[2]

# A Rising Anger

Seeking a change in his life, David enrolled at the College of
Great Falls, taking classes for an advanced degree in education.
In 1973, he completed his degree. He then moved to Lisbon,
Iowa, and became a high school English teacher.

In the meantime, Ted educated himself on wilderness living.
He studied hunting, gardening, and how to identify edible
plants as well as poisonous mushrooms. He filled his cabin with

books on these and other subjects. History and philosophy had been favorite areas of study since he was a teenager.

One book served as a personal touchstone: *The Technological Society* by the French philosopher Jacques Ellul. In this book, written in 1954, Ellul argued that machines and technology were changing humans to meet the constant demand for greater efficiency. Humans were accepting this change and helpless to stop it. In return, they received only the paltry benefit of modern comforts.

"The machine tends not only to create a new human environment, but also to modify man's very essence," Ellul wrote. "He must adapt himself, as though the world were new, to a universe for which he was not created."[3] That also meant there was a new definition for beauty in the world, Ellul said: that which is most efficient.

In his book, Ellul expressed what Kaczynski had long been thinking. Even in this remote spot, he couldn't escape machines and their noisy efficiency. Jets flew overhead, disrupting the peaceful quiet of Montana with their noise. In winter, snowmobiles churned through the woods, blasting artificial paths through the snow. Noisy motorcycles and off-trail bikes skittered past his cabin, and next door the Gehring sawmill buzzed and rumbled all day long.

It was too much for Kaczynski to bear, and it made him angry. He became upset enough to begin planning to lash

Ted's cabin had a small stove and shelves filled with books, food, and supplies.

out violently. While on his rambles through the woods, he met neighbors, including Cliff Gehring's son, Butch, and Chris Waits. Kaczynski would sometimes hunt for food on land Waits owned. Kaczynski borrowed tools from Gehring and Waits to build and maintain his cabin. He also scrounged material from nearby scrap heaps for a project that absorbed many of his waking hours: the making of bombs.

## Taking Action

Kaczynski grew angry with his family. He began writing letters to his parents blaming them for his isolation and his inability

to find a place in society. He accused them of pushing him to
succeed at one of the toughest schools in the country just for
the purpose of displaying his achievements as a badge of honor
for themselves.

Kaczynski's conclusion that technological progress was
ultimately destructive fed into his determination to take violent
action against it. He made it his goal to harm people who represented
the leading academic edge of science and technology. He spent
many hours at the Lincoln library, searching through books and directories for
potential victims.

The method for his violent attacks would be homemade explosives. He
set his workbench skills to use creating small bombs that would be disguised
as parcels for mailing. The bombs would be contained within
wooden boxes he would craft from scrap lumber. He would use
iron pipes to hold smokeless powder, which would be ignited

Kaczynski isolated himself almost completely. But he did keep in touch with his family and his brother through letters, which allowed him to freely express his thoughts and feelings. In one letter sent to his mother in 1991, Kaczynski explained why, exactly, he had decided to hole up in the Montana wilderness:

*Suppose that for a period of years whenever you touched—let us say—a banana, you got a severe electric shock. After that you would always be nervous around bananas, even if you knew they weren't wired to shock you. Well, in the same way, the many rejections, humiliations and other painful influence [sic] that I underwent during adolescence at home, in high school, and at Harvard have conditioned me to be afraid of people. . . . This fear of rejection—based on bitter experience both at home and at school—has ruined my life, except for the few years that I spent alone in the woods, largely out of contact with people.[5]*

to cause an explosion. The detonator would be sprung with some action by the receiver—either opening the package or manipulating the box in some way.

To build and mail explosives, Kaczynski decided he would have to travel. Sending everything from Lincoln would lead investigators straight to his cabin door. He would have to mail from places distant from his home. To travel to these places, he would need money. And to get money, he would need a job. With this plan in mind, in 1978 he returned, temporarily, to Chicago.

# CHAPTER FOUR

# REJECTION AND RAGE

n early 1978, Ted Kaczynski returned to Evergreen Park. He moved in with Turk and Wanda, as did David. All three of the Kaczynski men worked at Foam Cutting Engineers, a factory in Addison, another Chicago suburb. Having quit his job as a teacher, David became a supervisor to Ted and other workers at the factory.

His parents may have hoped Ted had returned to Chicago for good and would eventually settle down. But the older Kaczynski brother didn't have much interest in factory work and had no intention of staying in town. By holding down a job and living at home, he was simply trying to earn money.

In Montana, he had found that jobs were scarce. He had been able to land only short-term labor jobs, sometimes working for his neighbor Butch Gehring at his sawmill. But Ted

**His 1978 return to the densely populated Chicago area saw Ted carry out his first attack against the modern industrial world.**

needed materials for the projects he was working on at his cabin, and for that he simply needed to raise money.

## A Brief Friendship

It was at Foam Cutting Engineers that Ted met Ellen Tarmichael. There seemed to be a spark between them, and Ellen agreed to go out for dinner. On their next date, they baked pies at the Kaczynski home. But after this, Tarmichael broke off the relationship. She told Ted that they just didn't have much in common.

Ted didn't take it well. Much later, Ellen Tarmichael remembered him being civil about their brief romance. But he took revenge by writing insulting limericks about Tarmichael and posting them at the factory. For this, he was disciplined by his brother. When he ignored David and posted more insulting lines for the workers to see, David fired him. It was August 1978. Ted had already set his first homemade bomb on the ground at the University of Illinois, Chicago Circle. The next year, he moved back to Montana.

In May 1979, graduate student John Harris at Northwestern University found a package that looked like a cigar box in the school's Technical Building. Curious about the container, he opened it. The box exploded, and Harris suffered burns and cuts.

Kaczynski's second bomb, like his first, exploded at Northwestern University in Illinois.

That fall, Kaczynski prepared a new kind of bomb. In this device, the detonator was linked to an altimeter, a device that measures altitude. He placed it in a package that he intended to mail. This time, Kaczynski knew it would probably be carried to its destination aboard an airplane. When the aircraft reached a certain altitude, the altimeter would trigger the device to explode.

Kaczynski mailed the package, not knowing or caring which airplane would carry it. The bomb ended up in a mail carrier inside the cargo hold of American Airlines Flight 444, which took off from Chicago's O'Hare International Airport on November 15, 1979. As the Boeing 727 jet airliner was climbing to its cruising altitude, the bomb exploded.

There were 72 passengers aboard Flight 444, which was headed to Washington, DC.[2] The explosion caused a thumping noise, but at first the pilots and crew did not notice anything wrong. Some time later, smoke began seeping into the cabin of the plane from the cargo hold below. Flight attendants ordered passengers in front to the rear of the plane, away from the smoke. The pilots dropped the oxygen masks from their compartments so passengers could breathe. Meanwhile, the pilots guided the plane to an emergency landing at Dulles International, an airport in the Washington, DC, area.

The bomb was not strong enough to bring down the aircraft. But the fire damaged the cargo hold. Several of the passengers also suffered the effects of heavy smoke inhalation, though no one was killed.

# The Bomb in the Book

At his home in Montana, Kaczynski had an ongoing problem with the noise of airplanes. He had taken out his anger with a bomb, putting dozens of lives in danger aboard American Airlines Flight 444. He had packed enough explosives inside the device to take down the airplane. Fortunately for the passengers and crew, Kaczynski's bomb had malfunctioned, with the explosive powder merely smoldering rather than exploding.

In June 1980, Kaczynski sent a letter to Percy Wood, the president of United Airlines, who lived in Lake Forest, Illinois.

## GROWING ANGRY IN THE WOODS

Kaczynski never ended up finding the peace and solitude he craved in Lincoln, Montana. The noises of overhead planes, snowmobiles, and the neighboring sawmill enraged him. Worse, Butch Gehring had given his young daughter Jamie a small motorcycle. She loved to take the noisy machine through the woods on the small dirt trails that crisscrossed the forested hillsides.

Kaczynski recorded his rising anger in a diary he kept, writing about wanting to carry out violence against motorcycle riders who were disturbing him. Reading this much later, the passage made Jamie Gehring think about her strange, reclusive neighbor. She realized that her noisy Honda may have driven him into a rage and could have led to violent acts targeting her and her family.

Local police guarded the home of Percy Wood following the bombing.

The letter, signed "Enoch W. Fisher," promised that an important book would soon be coming in the mail. A week later, on June 10, Wood received a small package. Opening the parcel, he found it contained a copy of *Ice Brothers,* a novel by Sloan Wilson. He examined the book and then opened it.

Inside *Ice Brothers* was a rectangular cavity cut out of the pages. Within this space was a small explosive device. When Wood opened *Ice Brothers,* the book instantly detonated in his hands. Wood survived the explosion, although he was badly injured.

Kaczynski had not yet realized his goal of killing somebody with his homemade bombs. He had hurt several people and caused terror among passengers and crew on a commercial flight. But the bomb sent to Wood earned him something new: the attention of the FBI.

# Opening an Investigation

Established in the early decades of the 1900s, the FBI investigates interstate criminal activity, as well as terrorism carried out within the United States. During the 1970s, air terrorism was a major concern for the agency. There had been hijackings and attempts to bomb airplanes since the 1930s. But now, large passenger jets carrying hundreds of civilians had become frequent targets. The Flight 444 bomb was only the latest example.

Considering the similarities in the designs of the Wood bomb and the American Airlines device, the agency concluded that it might be dealing with a single dedicated bomber. Over the next several years, as the string of bombings continued, investigators compared data from the different incidents. Their intent was to come up with features common to all of them. Eventually, they would use these findings to work up a profile of the bomber and his methods. That would allow them to narrow down the range of suspects until, hopefully, a single individual could be identified.

Each different bomb, for example, had used a homemade initiator—the component that triggers the explosion. In the first bomb, the initiator was a bundled group of match heads. For some reason, perhaps to avoid the risk of making suspicious purchases, the Unabomber never used commercially available initiators, such as blasting caps.

Investigators also noted that the soldering of wires and metal components was poorly done. They observed that the Unabomber used poor-quality wood and scavenged boxes, such as old cigar boxes. This suggested that the bomber was probably working in a home workshop and not in any kind of commercial operation such as an explosives factory.

# CHAPTER FIVE

# THE MOUNTING TOLL

Kaczynski had found the small piece of wilderness he was seeking in Montana. He had built his own cabin and managed to survive from meat he hunted and vegetables he raised in a small garden. But he was still far from the life of independence and self-sufficiency he had imagined.

With no job and no income, Kaczynski had to borrow money from his family to buy materials from a local hardware store. For wood and scrap metal, he often spent nights rummaging through toolsheds, junked cars, scrap piles, and the small sawmill on the Gehring property. To build his homemade bombs, he needed matches, batteries, nails, and electrical wire. For explosives, he used various smokeless powders and sometimes metal shavings that he melted down over his wood-burning stove.

**Ted's isolation in the woods of Montana and his careful process helped him hide from the FBI for years.**

Much of his time was spent designing new bombs. He created schematics of these devices in a journal. Kaczynski wrote descriptions of them in Spanish, a language he had taught himself. Later, he created a number cipher for his diary entries. He also recorded the results of his work. When a bomb failed to go off or was disarmed, he felt disappointment. When people were injured or killed, he expressed satisfaction. As time went on, the bombs became stronger and more dangerous.

# Danger and Destruction

As the FBI searched for the Unabomber, Kaczynski worked to improve his devices. To throw investigators off his trail, he rode buses long distances to his target destinations. On October 8, 1981, Kaczynski arrived on the campus of the University of Utah in Salt Lake City. He walked to Milton Bennion Hall, a classroom building that also held a computer lab, and placed one of his packages.

Anna Wood managed Lincoln's small hardware store, and she became acquainted with Kaczynski.

The package sat in the hallway for some time with students walking past. Paul Larsen, a business student, stopped to pick up the package. There was a hole in the bottom and a spring dangling from the hole. Larsen put the package back on the ground and called the police.

Members of the university security department arrived. But the campus police did not have the equipment or the knowledge to deal with a suspected bomb. They cleared the hall and called a bomb disposal squad from the US Army's base at Fort Douglas, just east of Salt Lake City.

Carefully handling the package, the bomb squad examined it with a stethoscope and other devices. They spotted a long metal pipe filled with powder, along with a can of gasoline. Classes were evacuated and a fire alarm was set off. As the building was evacuated, the bomb squad brought the device upstairs into a women's restroom. They surrounded it with sandbags and set it off. Nobody was hurt.

The incident was reported to the FBI. Larsen had been lucky—the spring trigger on the bomb malfunctioned. The pipe bomb and the gasoline, if detonated, would have caused a deadly explosion and fireball.

In the next year, Kaczynski found two more targets. In May 1982, computer science professor Patrick Fischer received a package on the campus of Vanderbilt University in Nashville, Tennessee. Fischer had moved to Nashville after resigning his previous position at Penn State University. The package had

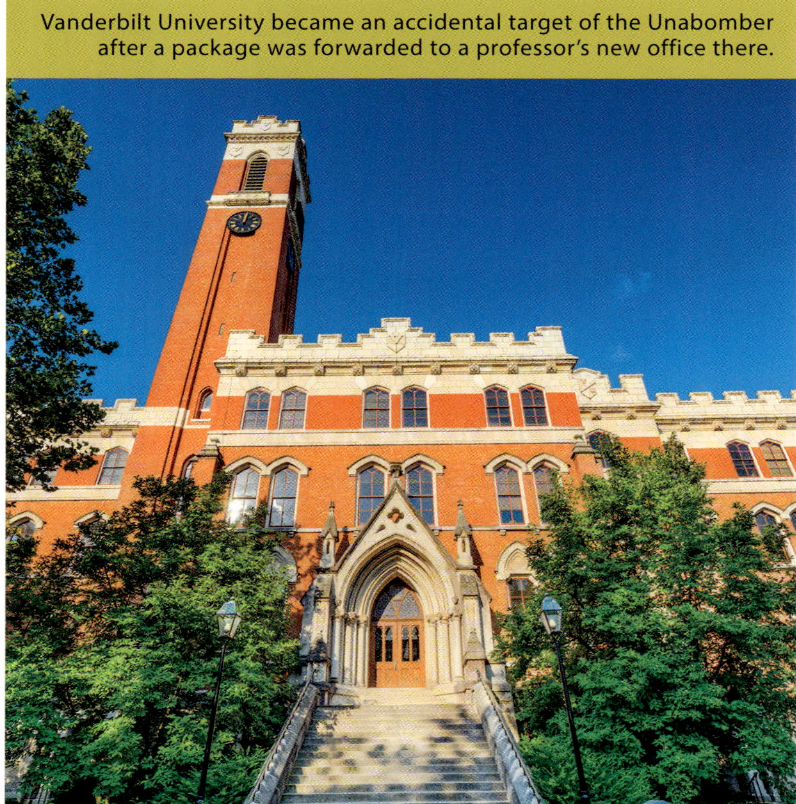

Vanderbilt University became an accidental target of the Unabomber after a package was forwarded to a professor's new office there.

been sent from Utah, addressed to him at Penn State and then forwarded to his new office.

Fischer was out of the office at the time, attending a conference in Puerto Rico. In his absence, his secretary, Janet Smith, opened the package. Inside was a pipe bomb made from a sink trap, a curved pipe used to collect water draining from a kitchen or bathroom sink. The bomb exploded, causing burns and cuts to Smith's upper body and arms, sending her to the hospital for three weeks.

Two months later, a mysterious package arrived at the University of California, Berkeley. The package made its way to a teacher's lounge inside Cory Hall, where somebody unwrapped it. A small silver cylinder showing a set of dials emerged from the packaging and was placed on a table. Diogenes Angelakos, a professor of electrical engineering, found the cylinder. Curious to figure out what it was, he picked it up from the table. The device exploded in his hands, showering his body with shards of metal shrapnel contained within the bomb. He was injured but not killed. A small note was found inside the box, typed on note paper. It said: "Wu, it works. I told you it would. RV."[1]

## The First Fatality

After the Berkeley bombing, the Unabomber was quiet for three years. Then, in 1985, he sent another package to Berkeley.

This package, like the first, found its way to Cory Hall.
On May 15, an engineering student picked up the device, which
exploded and caused severe but nonfatal injuries.

Investigators from the FBI arrived. The FBI Explosives Unit
had examined Kaczynski's devices, analyzing the explosives and
detonators, looking for fingerprints, and comparing designs.
But while the second Berkeley bomb was under investigation,
the agency received word that another mysterious package
had shown up in an office of the Boeing aircraft company in
Auburn, Washington.

At Boeing, FBI agents were led to a small mailed package
sitting on a table. For a month, the package had sat there while
office workers were careful not to disturb it. Finally, someone
had partially opened the package, discovered the bomb inside,
and called the FBI. Because the batteries had run down, they no
longer carried a charge and failed to detonate the explosives.
An FBI bomb squad detonated the device, and the explosion
destroyed any useful evidence.

In November, Kaczynski sent a booby-trapped package
to James McConnell, a biology professor at the University of
Michigan. When McConnell's assistant, Nick Suino, opened
the package, he found a letter from "Ralph C. Kloppenburg."
The letter asked for an opinion on a master's thesis that was
supposedly contained within the package. The letter pointed to
chapters 11 and 12 as particularly important. A bomb exploded

For years, the FBI studied the remains of the Unabomber's
explosives for potential clues.

as Suino handled the package, injuring both McConnell
and Suino.

In December, Kaczynski traveled to Sacramento, California,
with a package in hand. He walked to a parking lot behind
Century Plaza, a small strip mall. Several stores, including
RenTech, a shop that rented computer equipment, had back
doors onto the lot. He set the bomb down there.

Back home in his Montana cabin, Kaczynski later wrote:
"Experiment 97. Dec. 11, 1985, I planted bomb disguised to
look like scrap of lumber behind Rentech Computer Store

in Sacramento. According to San Francisio [sic] Examiner, Dec. 20, The 'operator' (owner? manager?) of the store was killed, 'blown to bits.'"[2]

This was Hugh Scrutton, who had either moved or picked up the package while it was lying on the ground. The explosion sent shrapnel flying into Scrutton's head and chest, as well as into the back wall of the shopping center. Scrutton died at a local hospital a short time later, the first fatality in the Unabomber case.

# Building a Profile

The FBI's UNABOM task force had its headquarters in San Francisco, California. For several years, the agency had been building a profile of its likely suspect. In the opinion of the FBI's profilers, their suspect held some kind of deep-seated anger at the academic world, as many of his targets had been universities. Based on the bombs directed at United Airlines and Boeing, he or she also seemed to have a grievance against the airline industry.

The UNABOM case was becoming one of the biggest, most expensive, and longest-running investigations in FBI history. There were special agents, explosives experts, profilers, section chiefs, and assistant directors involved. By the mid-1980s, all of them had tried and failed to find this single individual, who seemed to be very good at evading detection.

Then, in February 1987, the FBI got a significant break. In that month, two witnesses in Salt Lake City spotted a man walking through a parking lot behind another computer store, CAAMS. They saw the man place a wooden box on the ground. Later that morning, Gary Wright, the owner of CAAMS, drove into the lot. He stopped near the box and, feeling suspicious, got out and gave it a small kick. The box exploded, injuring Wright's arm.

## TED KACZYNSKI: THE PROFILE

FBI profilers work up detailed descriptions of unknown criminal suspects using every scrap of information available. They're more interested in personality than physical attributes. Their task is to identify the background, talents, interests, and motivations of criminals.

One of the agency's most famous profilers was John Douglas. Douglas was the first to profile the Unabomber. He described the Unabomber as a male in his late twenties or early thirties. The bomber had a background in the Chicago area and connections or experience in the academic world, and he was an "obsessive-compulsive loner of above average intelligence."[3]

Years later, Gary Wright revisited the Salt Lake City parking lot where he had been injured by the Unabomber's bomb.

The FBI investigated the incident. One of the witnesses had gotten a good look at the bomber. It had been a young adult male wearing a hooded sweatshirt and aviator sunglasses. But the sighting did not lead to any results.

## Lying Low

After the CAAMS bombing, Kaczynski slowed the pace of his work. He would remain quiet for the next seven years, although he continued designing and building explosive devices. In the meantime, multiple law enforcement agencies were working

the case, including the FBI's Laboratory Explosives Unit,
the Postal Inspection Service, and the Sacramento County
Sheriff's Office.

But FBI leadership was gradually losing patience. FBI agents
working the investigation got no good leads or tips in that
seven-year period. Many of the agents on the UNABOM case
believed there was a good chance the Unabomber, whoever he
might be, was dead. Perhaps he had been killed by one of his
own bombs. Or maybe he had been put in prison for a different
crime. But they were wrong, and eventually the Unabomber
would surface again.

# CHAPTER SIX

# A FRUITLESS SEARCH

To avoid detection, Kaczynski used commonly available materials in his handmade bombs. He was careful not to leave fingerprints or any other traces of his identity on his explosive devices. He mailed the deadly parcels from distant post offices so that postal inspectors could not trace them back to his home in Lincoln.

To throw investigators off his trail, he selected random targets that had no connection to each other or to him. He also mostly avoided pointing investigators to his own past. Instead of Harvard, he sent bombs to Northwestern and the University of Utah. His bombs had targeted airliners, private homes, and computer stores. He did, however, send two bombs to the University of California, Berkeley, where he had taught for two years.

**Kaczynski was a frequent visitor to the Lincoln Community Library, where he did research to identify potential targets.**

LINCOLN
COMMUNITY
LIBRARY

To find potential victims, he browsed material at the small Lincoln Community Library. Kaczynski made friends with librarian Sherri Wood, who helped him find useful reference books. One of these, *Who's Who in America,* was a directory of leading figures in politics, media, and the academic world, complete with career information and addresses. From *Who's Who*, Kaczynski chose a professor of genetics living in Tiburon, California, a small town on San Francisco Bay. For Kaczynski, college professors working in advanced scientific fields, including the medical frontier of genetics, were prime targets.

Meanwhile, Kaczynski was cutting off contact with his family. The last visit from his brother, David, had been in 1986. Letters passed back and forth from Montana to his brother and mother, but any attempt by his family to set up a meeting was met with an angry outburst. Ted often threatened to cut off the family entirely.

**After Ted Kaczynski's arrest, the Lincoln library became a prime destination for followers of the Unabomber story. Sherri Wood, the librarian, has met hundreds of tourists who show up and simply want to sit in the Unabomber's favorite chair or browse the same bookshelves he favored.**

At the UNABOM task force headquarters in San Francisco, FBI agents and supervisors were getting nowhere. The hunt for the Unabomber was scattered all over the country. The case remained cold into the early 1990s.

Kaczynski was able to outwit the FBI for 18 years. But he couldn't avoid leaving some clues as to who and where he was. One clue, for example, was revealed by the addresses the Unabomber wrote in his mailings. The Unabomber had used "Tiburon-Belvedere" while writing out Charles Epstein's address in California.

This was the official name of the post office serving the town of Tiburon, but the commonly used name was simply Tiburon. Searching through public records and directories, the FBI found that the only publication that showed Epstein's address this way was the 1992–93 edition of *Who's Who in America*. The FBI put together a list of all public libraries that held this reference book and then cross-checked this list with the bombing sites. Agents wondered whether some librarian, somewhere, might have been inadvertently aiding the Unabomber in his search for targets.

Some agents were assigned to other cases, where there seemed a much better chance of catching the perpetrators. But then, in 1993, two more bombs exploded.

# Bombings on the Coasts

At his home in Tiburon, geneticist Charles Epstein came home from a vacation to find a big pile of mail waiting for him on the dining room table. Among the flyers and envelopes, a heavy mailing envelope stuck out. Obviously, this was more than a letter—it looked as if it might hold a book. Picking it up, Epstein noticed a small pull tab on the package. It was designed to tear and open the package when the receiver pulled on it.

Epstein pulled, and the envelope exploded with a startling noise. Fragments of a copper tube, wood, switches, brackets,

Charles Epstein lost multiple fingers but managed
to survive the Unabomber's bomb.

and nine-volt batteries were propelled with sudden force
around the room. Shrapnel from the bomb tore into a dining
room chair, which the unsuspecting Epstein was standing
behind. The chair saved his life.

Across the country, a computer science professor at Yale
University in New Haven, Connecticut, received something
very similar in the mail. Professor David Gelernter opened the
envelope. The explosion sent bomb fragments into his chest
and head, and it blew off several fingers.

Both of these packages had been mailed from San Francisco
on the same day. The Unabomber had selected victims on the

West and East Coasts. His plan was to have the bombs reach their destinations and go off at about the same time—ideally on the same day. It had been several years since he had last sent a bomb through the mail. He may have wanted to cause maximum sensation in the news media and fear among the public.

Kaczynski also chose this moment to begin communicating with the media. He sent a letter to the *New York Times* claiming to be a member of a group known simply as FC. It had been mailed from Sacramento, where the Unabomber had also mailed the bombs to Gelernter and Epstein.

Knowing that the *Times* and other papers might be getting tips and communications from many other people, the sender had included a nine-digit number in the letter. He instructed the *Times* to keep this number secret and use it to verify any future letters or warnings that he chose to send. The Unabomber had begun to talk.

# Victimology

The FBI put together a victimology report. This was a collection of all data associated with the Unabomber's targets. The goal was to find some common link between all the victims. The agency also appealed to the public, offering a $1 million reward and setting up a toll-free number reserved exclusively for Unabomber tips. The FBI tried establishing a connection

David Gelernter recovered from his injuries, though he suffered permanent damage to his right hand.

between the Unabomber locations, including the bombing sites and the return addresses written on the packages. The search led them to conclude their suspect was someone from the academic world, perhaps a disgruntled student, professor, or college administrator.

The cross-checking was time-consuming and difficult. Agents assembled massive lists of people associated with these locations in an attempt to find one individual who had been present at all of them, at one time or another. They relied on driver's license records, property records, and other public records. Although the search did not yield any individual name, it narrowed down the suspects to someone who had moved from Chicago to the western states.

The FBI also decided to commission a new sketch. Jeanne Boylan, a well-known sketch artist, was put on the case. After interviewing the witness who briefly saw the Unabomber in 1987, she came up with a detailed drawing of the suspect. The FBI sent the sketch out to the press and television news, and soon the entire country had an image to link to the Unabomber.

In the meantime, Kaczynski was feeling proud of the havoc he was causing. He was not only outwitting the world's biggest law enforcement agency but also felt he was proving himself smarter than the smartest people in the country—academics at top research universities such as Berkeley and Yale. Back in his cabin, he made the following entry in his diary:

A new sketch of the Unabomber produced in 1994 became one of the most famous suspect sketches of all time.

*Dr. Gelernter: People with advanced degrees aren't as smart as they think they are. If you'd had any brains you would have realized that there are a lot of people out there who resent bitterly the way techno-nerds like you are changing the world and you wouldn't have been dumb enough to open an unexpected package from an unknown source.[1]*

# Thomas Mosser

December 1, 1994, was a proud day for Thomas J. Mosser. He became a general manager at Young & Rubicam, a big New York advertising firm. Having just reached 50 years of age, he was at the top of one of the biggest, most successful ad agencies in the world.

On the evening of Friday, December 9, the Mosser family was enjoying a typical weekend at the big house they had built in North Caldwell, a wealthy suburb in northern New Jersey. Several neighbor kids were playing in the house, having wandered over from a nearby house party to play with Mosser's 13-year-old daughter, Kim. They may not have noticed the package sitting on the dining room table.

On Saturday, December 10, Mosser found the package. Curious, he picked it up and started to open it. It exploded in his hands, and Mosser was killed instantly.



After the bombing death of Thomas Mosser at his home in North Caldwell, New Jersey, Kaczynski sent out the following message: "We blew up Thomas Mosser last December because he was a Burston-Marsteller executive. Among other misdeeds, Burston-Marsteller helped Exxon clean up its public image after the Exxon Valdez incident."[3] He was referencing the *Exxon Valdez*, an oil tanker that spilled millions of gallons of toxic oil and waste into the waters off Alaska in 1989. Kaczynski had misspelled the name of ad agency Burson-Marsteller. He was right that the agency had the oil company Exxon as a client. But at the time of his death, Mosser no longer worked for Burson-Marsteller.

# CHAPTER SEVEN

# THE MANIFESTO

n April 1995, a small package arrived at the office of the California Forestry Association. The street address in Sacramento, California, was correct. The name of the organization's president, which appeared on the mailing label, was not. William Dennison had left the job a year before. His replacement, Gilbert Murray, found the package addressed to Dennison lying on his desk.

Murray could have forwarded the package to Dennison, but he may have assumed it was forestry business. Whoever sent it could have been acting on old information, not realizing that Dennison was no longer the association's president. If they had known Dennison personally and this was some sort of gift, Murray may have reasoned, they would probably have sent it to Dennison's home address.

While unwrapping the package, Murray could not have realized what it contained—a powerful bomb. The explosion

**The wife and sons of Gilbert Murray dedicated a memorial to him a few years after he was the victim of the Unabomber's third fatal attack.**

Professional Forester's
Week—In Conservation
ornia's Natural Re
By Governor
th Day of

blew out the windows of his office, destroyed furniture, and rattled the entire one-story headquarters of the California Forestry Association. Murray was killed instantly.

# Explaining Himself

With two fatal bombings within the last year, Kaczynski now felt a need to explain himself. He completed a 35,000-word essay called "Industrial Society and Its Future" and sent it to the *New York Times* and the *Washington Post*. If these papers agreed to publish his work, he promised, then he would stop sending bombs through the mail.

The newspapers immediately notified the FBI. Reading the manifesto and the accompanying letter, FBI director Louis Freeh and Attorney General Janet Reno realized they had an important decision to make. The FBI would not normally release communications

Attorney General Janet Reno and other law enforcement officials carefully considered whether to print the Unabomber's manifesto.

such as this to the public. In the agency's view, it was a way of rewarding criminal activity and didn't do their investigations any good.

But the Unabomber case was unique. The bomber had been on his deadly spree for 17 years, and the FBI wasn't much closer to finding and arresting a suspect than they had been at the start. At this point, the investigation had reached a dead end. If the Unabomber's manifesto were published, on the other hand, there was a possibility that someone, somewhere might recognize something in it. A friend, a colleague, an employer, or a relative might see familiar ideas, phrases, or even misspellings.

The decision to publish the manifesto was a last-ditch effort by the FBI to find a new lead in the case.

The UNABOM task force recommended that the manifesto be published. It was a chance Freeh decided to take. He persuaded Reno to go along with the plan.

# The Manifesto Appears

"Industrial Society and Its Future" was published on September 19, 1995. It appeared as a supplementary section included with that day's edition of the *Washington Post*. The *Post* had agreed to split the cost of publication with the *New York Times*, which didn't have the equipment to print the manifesto section on short notice.

In his manifesto, Kaczynski spelled out his many problems with scientific progress. In his view, the forward march of technology meant increasing limits on human freedom. Society was turning into a vast consumer market for large corporations. Companies were motivated solely by profit and not at all by what humans actually needed, which was to be in control of their own goals and destinies.

In 2011, the Swiss illustrator Valentín Ramón Menendez released a graphic novel adaptation of "Industrial Society and Its Future."

He wrote, "Advertising and marketing techniques have been developed that make many people feel they need things that their grandparents never desired or even dreamed of." He held a bleak view of the future if nothing was done to slow down or stop the improvement of machines and automation: "In that case presumably all work will be done by vast, highly organized systems of machines and no human effort will be necessary."[2]

In response, he said he felt compelled to slow down or stop this dangerous progress. He recognized this struggle would bring pain to many but thought the ultimate goal was worth the suffering. Kaczynski gave his readers a concise explanation for his own actions: "To make an impression on society with words is therefore almost impossible for most individuals and small groups. . . . In order to get our message before the public with some chance of making a lasting impression, we've had to kill people."[3]

He also said there was another solution to the problems of technology and progress. The solution didn't involve violence or harming anybody. It meant returning to the wilderness and living as human beings were meant to live. Kaczynski wrote, "Nature makes a perfect counter-ideal to technology for several reasons. Nature (that which is outside the power of the system) is the opposite of technology (which seeks to expand indefinitely the power of the system). . . . To relieve the pressure on nature it is not necessary to create a special kind of social system, it is only necessary to get rid of industrial society."[4]

Kaczynski may have thought he needed to explain the reason for the violence, death, and fear he had unleashed from his solitary cabin. He may have wanted to convince people that modern society was headed for disaster and that to avoid this disaster, humans would have to adopt a new mode of life. He may also have thought it useful to get the essay published widely so that people could read it and act on it.

However, the Unabomber's manifesto had another effect, and it was not something Kaczynski had intended. It eventually led investigators straight to his cabin door. And the most important people that the words had reached were not world leaders or people of influence. They were Kaczynski's own brother and his brother's wife.

## Troubling Thoughts

It was a troubled statement by Linda Patrik, Kaczynski's sister-in-law, that started the investigation that would end with the capture of the Unabomber. "David," she said, "don't be

Kaczynski wrote out a draft of his manifesto by hand.

angry with me."[6] She was speaking to her husband, David Kaczynski. It was the summer of 1995, a time when the Unabomber was terrorizing the country with his deadly bombs. The story was all over television and in the newspapers. Every time a new bomb went off, intense coverage began again and lasted several days. "Has it ever occurred to you," Linda asked, "even as a remote possibility, that your brother might be the Unabomber?"[7]

Something about these events had been giving Linda a bad feeling. For some reason, the Unabomber reminded her of her brother-in-law. She hadn't met him, but she saw him as a strange and angry person. It seemed possible that he would try to harm others. Now she had to say something.

# UNABOMBER ATTACKS BY STATE

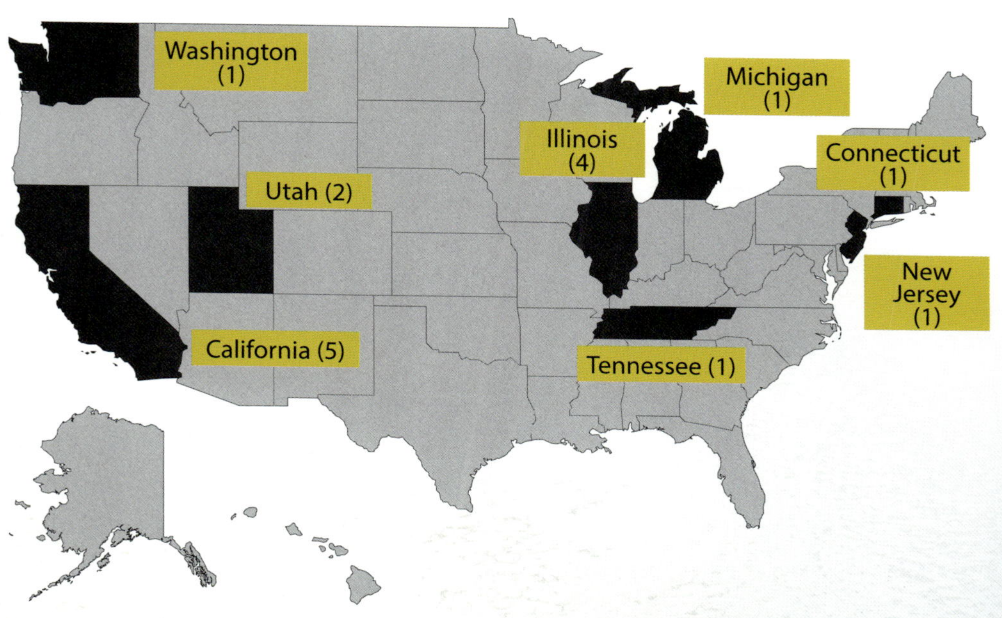


The Unabomber's attacks were spread out across the country, making it difficult for investigators to tell where the attacker was based.

# LYING IN WAIT

At first, David Kaczynski couldn't or wouldn't believe it. His brother was a bit strange and certainly antisocial. Ted also had serious problems with modern technology and felt a deep contempt for the society around him. But Ted was not unique in these feelings. A lot of people lived in the woods and didn't care to join the mainstream.

When the brothers were growing up and going to college, many in their generation were dropping out and seeking a simpler life. They didn't bomb or kill, and as far as David knew, Ted had never been violent. Ted didn't harm people or animals, he didn't travel, and he had no money. He depended on money from his family to pay for medical care when he needed it.

But David had to admit that there were some curious coincidences. For one, a professor at the University of California, Berkeley, had been targeted. For a couple of years, Ted had taught mathematics classes at Berkeley. There had also been

FBI agent Max Noel, an investigator in the UNABOM case, sifted through vast amounts of evidence in the years leading up to the 1995 breakthrough.

WRITINGS
UNABOMER LETTERS
UNABOM LETTERS/LABELS/STAMPS
UNABOM
DETAILED PHOTOGRAPHS OF DEVICES #11 AND #12 BY CABIN TECH TWITER
ACTS OF VANDALISM
149A-SF-106204 SUB S-2416
UNABOM
MAJOR CASE 75
SSA Noel
UNABOM
NABOM
PHOTOGRAPHS
DEVICE #11 AND DEVICE #12
VOLUME 2

bombings in Chicago, the area where the Kaczynski brothers grew up.

Then, in the fall of 1995, the manifesto appeared. David and Linda read the document on the internet. David hoped reading the Unabomber manifesto would allow him to dismiss Linda's suspicions. Instead, it did just the opposite.

The document contained eerie similarities to Ted's writing style, which David knew from the many letters he had received. Ted, like the author of the manifesto, wrote some words with British spellings, such as "analyse" instead of "analyze." "Cool-headed logicians" was one of Ted's favorite phrases, and it appeared in the manifesto.[1] Ted and the manifesto author also used the phrase "eat your cake and have it too." This was an inversion of the more common phrase "have your cake and

## MOVING ABROAD

With the publication of "Industrial Society and Its Future" and his arrest in 1996, Ted Kaczynski became notorious outside as well as within the United States. In 2011, supporters of the Unabomber in Mexico established an "eco-terrorist" group known as Individualidades Tendiendo a lo Salvaje (ITS), or Individualists Tending toward the Wild. The members believe that Kaczynski's plan to use violence to bring down modern society was the right idea but was moving too slowly.

ITS sent mail bombs to banks, universities, and the Mexican national electricity commission. In 2017, branches in South America began their own campaign of terror. One important target was Óscar Landerretche, the chairman of Codelco, the largest copper mining company in the world. Landerretche survived the bomb with minor injuries.

David's reading of the manifesto suggested his brother might be the Unabomber, but he knew he would need to proceed carefully before going to the FBI.

eat it too."[2] And of course, the manifesto's point that modern technology was harmful to society at large, and a return to living off the land was the solution, was something Ted had been saying for many years.

David struggled, not knowing what to do. He finally hit on the idea of visiting his brother. He would offer to drive out to Montana, stop in the city of Helena, and pick up any supplies Ted might need. When he arrived, he could try to figure out the truth: Was Ted making and sending bombs from Lincoln, or was he not?

The answer to his letter came about two weeks later. It was then that David realized his brother had gone over the edge into outright rage. As for any visit, Ted angrily told David not to bother. "I just get choked with frustration at my inability to get our stinking family off my back once and for all," he wrote. "I DON'T EVER WANT TO SEE YOU OR HEAR FROM YOU, OR ANY OTHER MEMBER OF OUR FAMILY, AGAIN."[3]

# Reading for Clues

The FBI had been on the Unabomber case since 1979. Over the years, the agency had received thousands of anonymous tips. By 1995, a $1 million reward was being offered for information leading to the arrest of the Unabomber.[4] It was the largest reward in the history of criminal justice. But neither the tips nor the reward money had led to an arrest.

David was concerned that simply calling the FBI wasn't good enough. He worried that his tip—that his brother might be the author of the manifesto—would be written down, filed away, and then forgotten. David felt he would first have to do an investigation of his own.

He hired Susan Swanson, a private investigator based in Chicago. Swanson, an old friend of Linda's, studied Ted's letters and writings. She then got in touch with Clint Van Zandt, a former member of the FBI who specialized in behavioral science. Swanson turned over typed copies of the letters to Van Zandt. She gave him no information about the author or about the Kaczynski brothers.

Van Zandt then set up two independent teams to analyze the letters. One team was made up of two experts in the field of communications. The other was made up of a psychiatrist and a language expert. The goal was to develop two independent opinions on the possibility that the letter writer and the manifesto author were the same person.

The two teams compared language, spelling, and grammar. Both teams came to the same conclusion. They felt the chances were likely that the author of the letters and the author of the manifesto were the same person. Van Zandt then passed along some advice: whoever submitted these letters should contact the FBI. But Swanson was still concerned that simply calling the tip line wouldn't get them anywhere.

Swanson then got in touch with a former law school classmate, Anthony Bisceglie. Now a lawyer in Washington, DC, Bisceglie had contacts inside the FBI. Without disclosing the name of Ted Kaczynski, Bisceglie reported to the agency that he might have a lead on the Unabomber. The FBI listened and acted.

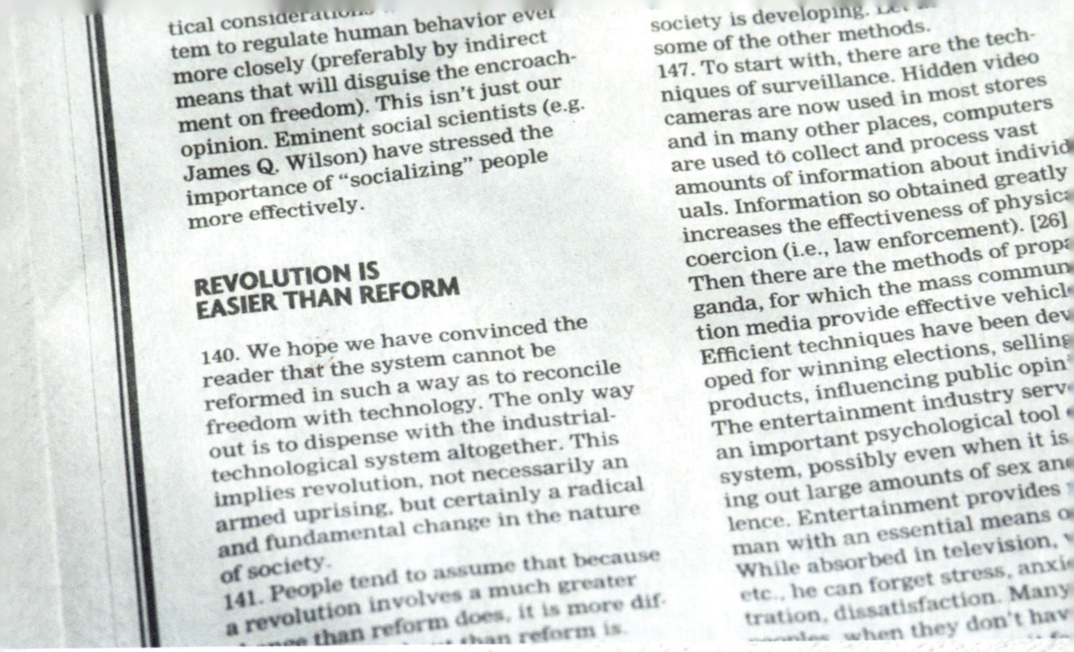

tical considerations ...
tem to regulate human behavior ever
more closely (preferably by indirect
means that will disguise the encroach-
ment on freedom). This isn't just our
opinion. Eminent social scientists (e.g.
James Q. Wilson) have stressed the
importance of "socializing" people
more effectively.

**REVOLUTION IS
EASIER THAN REFORM**

140. We hope we have convinced the
reader that the system cannot be
reformed in such a way as to reconcile
freedom with technology. The only way
out is to dispense with the industrial-
technological system altogether. This
implies revolution, not necessarily an
armed uprising, but certainly a radical
and fundamental change in the nature
of society.
141. People tend to assume that because
a revolution involves a much greater
... than reform does, it is more dif-
... than reform is.

society is developing. ...
some of the other methods.
147. To start with, there are the techniques of surveillance. Hidden video
cameras are now used in most stores
and in many other places, computers
are used to collect and process vast
amounts of information about individ
uals. Information so obtained greatly
increases the effectiveness of physic
coercion (i.e., law enforcement). [26]
Then there are the methods of propa
ganda, for which the mass commun
tion media provide effective vehicl
Efficient techniques have been dev
oped for winning elections, selling
products, influencing public opin
The entertainment industry serv
an important psychological tool
system, possibly even when it is
ing out large amounts of sex an
lence. Entertainment provides
man with an essential means o
While absorbed in television,
etc., he can forget stress, anxi
tration, dissatisfaction. Many
when they don't hav

Carefully studying the manifesto helped convince investigators that
Kaczynski was a likely suspect.

David did not want his name disclosed to the FBI or to the
media. He had good reasons to keep his secret. If his identity
got out, reporters would swarm his house, try to interview
him, and then write up his story. Ted would find out soon
enough that he was the target of an investigation. David knew
his brother, if forewarned, could get rid of any incriminating
evidence in his cabin and evade FBI agents coming to Lincoln.
Any hunt for him in the wilderness of Montana and beyond
would fail.

# The Stakeout

Through Bisceglie, David provided 86 letters he had received
over the years from his brother.[5] He also sent the agency a
23-page essay Ted had written in the early 1970s.[6] The essay

called for the end of funding of scientific research by the government and by corporations.

In order to protect Ted and the Kaczynski family if he ended up being innocent, Bisceglie kept David's name under wraps. When it received the documents, the FBI assigned James Fitzgerald to do a language analysis of the writings. Closely examining the documents, Fitzgerald checked similarities in spelling, grammar, and idioms. Altogether, Fitzgerald noted 160 such similarities between the manifesto and the anonymous documents.[7]

David and Bisceglie met face-to-face with law enforcement for the first time in February 1996. But before David could reveal the identity of the suspect, agents already realized that it must be David's older brother, Ted. The agency prepared teams for travel to Lincoln, Montana.

Using false identities, two teams checked into two different hotels in the small town. The teams

In its long hunt for the Unabomber, the FBI identified, tracked, and numbered each suspect. By the time it found Ted Kaczynski, the bureau had already gathered quite a few—Kaczynski was suspect number 2,416.[9]

watched traffic pass up and down Stemple Pass Road, the road leading to Ted's cabin about four miles (6.4 km) south of town.[8] To get closer, one of the teams later rented a small cabin on a bluff overlooking Kaczynski's cabin.

Surveillance teams watched Kaczynski as he puttered in and around the cabin. Listening devices were planted in the nearby woods. The agents used high-powered binoculars to keep a watch on Kaczynski. Surveillance aircraft and satellites flew overhead, keeping cameras focused on the area.

In late March, the FBI got a call from CBS, a major television network. Just as the FBI had feared, the media had heard of the story. Someone within the agency had, accidentally or on purpose, leaked the information that the FBI had a lead on the Unabomber.

CBS wanted confirmation that the agency was about to make an arrest in the case. The FBI offered no information but asked the network not to make the story public for now. CBS agreed—but time was now working against the stakeout

and the agents lying in
wait in Montana. Sooner
or later, CBS or another
network might go public
with the story to get
a scoop.



In the meantime, the FBI was working with federal
prosecutors in San Francisco to prepare a search warrant for the
cabin. The prosecutors wrote up a long affidavit. This was an
account of the FBI's actions in the case and a summary of the
evidence against Kaczynski. The affidavit had to be ready for a
judge to sign before the agency could search the cabin or make
an arrest.

On April 1, CBS called the FBI again. Two other networks,
CNN and ABC, now had the story and were preparing to make it
public. Time had run out.

The FBI pulled together two SWAT teams and flew them
to Helena. That evening, Terry Turchie, the FBI lead on the
Unabomber investigation, put the final touches on the affidavit.
In the early morning hours of April 3, Turchie brought the
affidavit to Judge William Lovell. As soon as the judge signed
the search warrant, Turchie radioed the agents waiting in
Lincoln. It was time to move in.

# CHAPTER NINE

# ON TRIAL

Standing near Kaczynski's rustic cabin, Forest Service officer Jerry Burns called out to him on the morning of April 3, 1996. "Ted, are you home?"[1] Knowing that Kaczynski was an acquaintance of Burns, the FBI had recruited the Forest Service officer for the arrest, hoping to prevent a dangerous standoff or a violent shootout.

A heavily armed tactical team waited in the woods and on the Gehring property nearby. Burns and two FBI agents with him listened as their suspect shifted around inside the cabin. Kaczynski finally came to the door. Realizing what was happening, he tried to duck back inside.

Burns grabbed him by the wrist. The agents handcuffed Kaczynski and led him outside. As their suspect was put into a waiting car, FBI agents swarmed the cabin and the grounds nearby. After a pursuit lasting almost two decades, the hunt for the Unabomber was finally over.

**Kaczynski was brought to Helena to be formally informed of the charges against him the day after his arrest.**

# The Search

Later that day, Kaczynski was flown to a holding cell in Sacramento, California. Meanwhile, with their search warrant in hand, FBI agents began carefully picking through the dark and cluttered cabin. The bureau had assigned one of the agents, explosives expert Donald Sachtleben, to look for any explosive devices either under construction or completed.

The goal was to find and preserve any evidence for a trial. Knowing that the Unabomber had left almost no traces of his identity, the agents were searching for anything that would connect Kaczynski to the bombings. They didn't have to look for very long.

Three-ring binders were found with detailed diagrams and notes, written in English and Spanish, for various homemade bombs. Kaczynski had also collected chemical formulas and recipes for explosive materials. In the cabin were containers for the raw ingredients: potassium chlorate, sodium chlorate, aluminum, zinc, lead, sugar, and silver oxide. Kaczynski had also collected several textbooks on electricity and chemistry.

Also found were ingots and shavings of aluminum, showing that the ingots had been filed

**The National Postal Museum in Washington, DC, owns and displays the set of handcuffs used to arrest Kaczynski at his Montana cabin on April 3, 1996.**

down to create the small filings that could be used in place of gunpowder. Kaczynski also had batteries, electrical wire, drills, hacksaws, wire cutters, and solder used to fashion electrical connections.

Finally, a wrapped package was found and x-rayed. Inside was a completed pipe bomb.



The pipe was sealed at both ends, meaning the explosive had already been inserted and was prepared for a detonator. But the device had a complicated system of wires and components that no one had ever seen before.

Without a bomb disposal expert up to the task, the FBI called in Chris Cherry of the Sandia National Laboratories in New Mexico to analyze and disarm the bomb. Considered one of the country's best bomb-disposal experts, Cherry could usually handle an explosive device in the space of a few hours. The Unabomber's last device took Cherry more than a week to dismantle.

## The Charges

In June, a federal attorney filed charges. Kaczynski was accused of transporting an explosive device with intent to kill or injure, mailing an explosive device with intent to kill or injure, and

Investigators found Kaczynski's final bomb in his cabin.

using an explosive device in a crime of violence. If found guilty of the first or second charge, the law allowed for a long prison sentence or the death penalty. For the third charge, the law set a mandatory sentence of 30 years in prison.

Kaczynski intended to plead not guilty to the charges. When a defendant makes such a plea, the court must schedule a trial. But Kaczynski had no money to pay lawyers. In this case, the law allows public defenders to represent those accused of serious crimes.

Kaczynski's court-appointed lawyers were allowed to review all the evidence the FBI had collected from the cabin. They realized that the government had a solid case against their client. They would probably lose in court, and their client might be subject to execution. Attorney General Janet Reno, the top law enforcement official in the federal government, announced that the Department of Justice would be seeking the death penalty.

To avoid a death sentence, Kaczynski's lawyers wanted their client to plead insanity. They would argue that Kaczynski was not mentally sound enough at the time of the crime to distinguish right from wrong. The court might allow him to live, although he would be sentenced to a long term, probably a life sentence.

To succeed, the lawyers needed a diagnosis from a medical professional. They hired several psychiatrists to examine Kaczynski. The doctors all found that Kaczynski likely had paranoid schizophrenia. Because he had a mental illness, in this view, he could not be held fully responsible for his actions.

## PRESIDENT UNABOMBER?

Even before Kaczynski was identified and arrested, a "Unabomber for President" campaign was underway. The campaign's leaders urged people to write in "Unabomber" on their presidential ballots for the 1996 election. The campaign was taken up by several antitechnology groups who believed in the message that technology had gone too far. The Unabomber Political Action Committee (UNAPACK) was also formed to raise money. The campaign didn't get far, however, and Bill Clinton won the 1996 election. The number of votes written in for Kaczynski was never tabulated. After the election, UNAPACK stayed in business. The group raised money by selling bumper stickers that said, "Don't Blame Me, I Voted for the Unabomber."[3]

Kaczynski was escorted under heavy guard to the federal courthouse in San Francisco in early 1998.

This defense seemed to have a good chance of standing up in court. The major problem with it, however, was Kaczynski himself. He did not agree with the diagnosis. In his opinion, he was fully in control of his senses and responsible for his actions. He did not admit any mental problems or illnesses. He did not want "Industrial Society and Its Future" to be dismissed as the ravings of a madman.

Jury selection in the case began on November 12, 1997, and lasted until December 22. At the end of this process, Judge Garland Burrell called for a meeting with the defense team. Kaczynski had submitted a request to the court. He intended to fire his lawyers, as he had no intention of pleading insanity.

The court denied his request. In January 1998, with the trial set to begin with opening statements, Kaczynski again asked Judge Burrell to allow him to fire his defense team and represent himself in court. Burrell again denied the request.

## Sentence

Dissatisfied with the reports of the previous psychiatrists, Judge Burrell brought in another psychiatrist, Sally Johnson, who worked for the Federal Bureau of Prisons. After an examination of Kaczynski, Johnson found that he was competent to stand trial, although she also explained she had made a "provisional" diagnosis of paranoid schizophrenia.[4] On January 22, Burrell then announced he had made an important decision in the case.

The judge reasoned that Kaczynski, in asking to represent himself, was only trying to delay the trial. Judge Burrell may have also feared the trial and his courtroom turning into a media spectacle. In another recent case in California, former football star O. J. Simpson had been charged for the murder of his ex-wife, Nicole Brown. The Simpson trial had become a national obsession. Newspapers and broadcast media reported the events of the trial by day and debated those same events every evening. The judge in Simpson's case, Lance Ito, was widely portrayed in the media as weak and incompetent for letting the proceedings get out of hand.

Judge Burrell and everyone in his Sacramento courtroom knew about the Simpson case. The judge may not have wanted

# UNABOMBER ATTACKS BY DATE

| DATE | LOCATION | VICTIMS |
| --- | --- | --- |
| May 25, 1978 | Northwestern University, Illinois | 1 injured |
| May 9, 1979 | Northwestern University, Illinois | 1 injured |
| November 15, 1979 | American Airlines Flight 444 | 12 injured |
| June 10, 1980 | Private home, Lake Forest, Illinois | 1 injured |
| October 8, 1981 | University of Utah | Bomb defused |
| May 5, 1982 | Vanderbilt University, Tennessee | 1 injured |
| July 2, 1982 | University of California, Berkeley | 1 injured |
| May 15, 1985 | University of California, Berkeley | 1 injured |
| June 13, 1985 | Boeing offices, Auburn, Washington | Bomb defused |
| November 15, 1985 | University of Michigan | 2 injured |
| December 11, 1985 | Computer store, Sacramento, California | 1 dead |
| February 20, 1987 | Computer store, Salt Lake City, Utah | 1 injured |
| June 22, 1993 | Private home, Tiburon, California | 1 injured |
| June 24, 1993 | Yale University, Connecticut | 1 injured |
| December 10, 1994 | Private home, North Caldwell, New Jersey | 1 dead |
| April 24, 1995 | California Forestry Association office, Sacramento, California | 1 dead |

his courtroom to turn into another media circus or himself to be portrayed as the next Lance Ito. For that reason, he denied Kaczynski's request to represent himself. Not willing to stand trial with the defense lawyers he had, Kaczynski then agreed to plead guilty to the charges.

## Prison Life

Sentencing took place on May 4, 1998. The court ordered Kaczynski to serve eight life terms without the possibility of parole. He was then sent to US Penitentiary, Administrative Maximum Facility, in Florence, Colorado—commonly known as ADX Florence. This ultrasecure prison, also known as "Supermax," is where some of the nation's most dangerous and notorious criminals are held.

In some ways, the high-security prison was a step up from Kaczynski's previous life. His cell was about the same size as his Montana cabin, but



Although he never married and had no girlfriends, Kaczynski made one close female friend while in prison. This was Joy Richards, a fourth-grade teacher who began writing to him soon after his trial. Richards and Kaczynski exchanged letters, poems, artwork, and music. Richards served as a person through whom he could communicate with the media and his family. In 2003, Kaczynski sold his 1.4-acre (0.6 ha) Montana property to the woman he called his "lady love."[5] Richards died from lung cancer in 2006.

unlike the cabin, it offered running water, heat, and electricity. Although Supermax prisoners live in solitary quarters, Kaczynski had some contact with prison guards and visitors, and he coped with his isolation by reading books and writing letters. He remained at the ADX facility until 2021, when for health reasons he was transferred to the Federal Medical Center in Butner, North Carolina. Kaczynski died there on June 10, 2023, at age 81.

Although he was incarcerated for decades, the Unabomber was not forgotten. "Industrial Society and Its Future" took on a life of its own after the trial and sentencing. It appeared in magazines, newspapers, and several book editions and was taken seriously by many reviewers as well as scientists, philosophers, intellectuals, and academics. The questions it raised about modern technology and its ill effects and dangers remain a common theme among contemporary observers of American society.

Some members of the environmental movement also took Kaczynski for an important thinker, writer, and leader. In 1997, even before Kaczynski was sentenced, the slogan "Free Ted Kaczynski"

**Kaczynski's literary works didn't stop with "Industrial Society and Its Future." He also wrote and published the books *Technological Slavery* and *Anti-Tech Revolution* from prison.**

appeared on a flyer circulated at a gathering of the Earth First! movement, which strives to halt economic development and the degradation of wilderness areas within the United States. "It may be that the Unabomber will be looked upon . . . as a kind of warrior-prophet," proclaimed the document.[6]

## The Unabomber's Impact

During his stay at ADX Florence, Kaczynski received many letters from supporters and others who had adopted his antitechnology philosophy. He corresponded with several leaders of the green anarchist movement, including author John Zerzan, who believes humans should return to their prehistoric life as hunter-gatherers. Kaczynski also granted media interviews, giving the first to Theresa Kintz of the *Green Anarchist*, a journal based in London. He also kept up correspondence with thousands of people who were simply curious about his motives and his views on current events.

There's little doubt that many people feel alienated in a world in which technology dominates. With the growth of online surveillance, data mining, and malicious hacking, technology has also come to feel somewhat threatening for many people. For some, artificial intelligence raises fears of a future in which human beings aren't even necessary. Some people feel sympathetic to the Unabomber's self-isolation and rage at rapid technological change.

Many others who were directly involved in the Unabomber story, either as investigators or as victims, have a very different take. When Unabomber target David Gelernter heard that the government was auctioning Kaczynski's personal belongings and using the money to compensate the victims, all he could feel was anger. "I find the idea of the auction revolting, sickening, profoundly despicable," Gelernter told a reporter from the *Yale Daily News*. "At the same time, I would love to see [some of the victims] get some restitution . . . not that any restitution can possibly repair a universe shattered through the criminal villainy of this murderer."[7]

## THE ITALIAN UNABOMBER

Kaczynski's bombings have inspired several copycats. One of the most active was an Italian bomber who was never caught. Working in northern Italy from 1994 until 2006, the criminal known as the "Italian Unabomber" placed booby-trap bombs in public areas. The Italian police attributed more than 30 incidents to him or her over a period of 12 years.[8] Several people were seriously injured. The Italian Unabomber never wrote any kind of manifesto and seemed to act out of pure malice. Police did make an arrest in the case, naming 49-year-old engineer Elvo Zornitta as their suspect in 2006. But with little solid evidence, prosecutors dropped the case. Since that time, the Italian Unabomber has gone quiet.

# TIMELINE

## 1942
- Ted Kaczynski is born in Chicago, Illinois, to Theodore "Turk" and Wanda Kaczynski on May 22. The family later moves to Evergreen Park, a Chicago suburb.

## 1958
- Kaczynski enters Harvard University as a 16-year-old freshman.

## 1962
- Kaczynski graduates with a bachelor's degree from Harvard University and enrolls in the graduate mathematics program at the University of Michigan.

## 1967
- Kaczynski is awarded a PhD in mathematics from the University of Michigan for his doctoral thesis on boundary functions. That fall, he accepts a teaching position at the University of California, Berkeley.

## 1969
- Kaczynski resigns from his teaching position at the University of California, Berkeley, and decides to give up his career in academia.

## 1971
- David and Ted Kaczynski buy a 1.4-acre (0.6 ha) parcel along Stemple Pass Road, a few miles south of Lincoln, Montana.

## 1978
- Kaczynski places his first parcel bomb in a parking lot on the University of Illinois Chicago Circle campus. The bomb eventually wounds a security guard at Northwestern University.

## 1979
- A second bomb is left in a room at Northwestern, injuring a student, and another malfunctions while being transported aboard an American Airlines passenger jet, forcing an emergency landing.

## 1980
- A bomb enclosed in a book injures Percy Wood, president of United Airlines.

## 1981
- A bomb is discovered and disarmed at the University of Utah in Salt Lake City.

# 1982

- Bombs cause injuries at the University of California, Berkeley, and Vanderbilt University in Nashville, Tennessee.

# 1985

- Three bombs detonate, while an additional bomb sent to the Boeing aircraft company in Auburn, Washington, is disarmed. One of the bombs kills Hugh Scrutton, a computer store owner in Sacramento, California.

# 1987

- A witness sees a man leave a bomb in the parking lot of a computer store in Salt Lake City. The witness's description allows the FBI to create a sketch of the Unabomber.

# 1993

- Bombs injure a geneticist at the University of California and a computer scientist at Yale University.

# 1994

- Thomas Mosser, a New Jersey marketing executive, is killed by a bomb sent to his home.

# 1995

- A bomb mailed to the California Forestry Association kills the organization's president, Gilbert Murray.

# 1996

- On April 3, Kaczynski is arrested at his cabin.

# 1998

- Kaczynski pleads guilty to the charges and is sentenced to eight life terms without parole. He is incarcerated at a maximum-security prison in Florence, Colorado.

# 2021

- For undisclosed medical reasons, Kaczynski is moved to a federal prison in Butner, North Carolina.

# 2023

- Kaczynski dies in prison on June 10 at age 81.

# ESSENTIAL FACTS

## SIGNIFICANT EVENTS

- Kaczynski's first targeted bomb goes off on the campus of Northwestern University on May 25, 1978, injuring campus police officer Terry Marker.

- Kaczynski's final victim, timber lobbyist Gilbert Murray, is killed by a bomb in his Sacramento office on April 24, 1995.

- On September 19, 1995, the *Washington Post* publishes Kaczynski's 35,000-word antitechnology manifesto, "Industrial Society and Its Future."

- FBI agents raid Kaczynski's Montana cabin on April 3, 1996, arresting him for various federal crimes related to his bombing campaign.

- On January 22, 1998, Kaczynski pleads guilty to the charges against him in a federal court in Sacramento, California. At his sentencing, he is ordered to serve eight life terms without parole.

## KEY PLAYERS

- Ted Kaczynski, raised in a middle-class suburban family, was a brilliant mathematician whose rage at modern technology transformed him into an antisocial recluse and then a murderous long-distance bomber.

- David Kaczynski, the younger brother of Ted, tipped off the FBI to the possibility that Ted might be the Unabomber.

- Linda Patrik, the wife of David Kaczynski, persuaded her husband to consider the possibility that his brother was actually the Unabomber.

- James Fitzgerald, a criminal profiler with the FBI, took the lead in analyzing the language of the Unabomber manifesto and matching it with letters and other writings of Ted Kaczynski.

- Judge Garland Burrell presided over the trial of Ted Kaczynski. He denied Kaczynski's request to defend himself at trial, prompting Kaczynski to plead guilty to the charges.

# IMPACT ON SOCIETY

The Unabomber's string of bombings held the country in fearful suspense for 18 years as the FBI failed to solve the case, the attacks grew in intensity, and two shocking long-distance killings took place over a span of five months. The Unabomber manifesto revealed that anger at the harms of modern technology was motivating the attacks.

An academic with a promising career as a university professor, Kaczynski had dropped out of society and lived in isolation. His goal was to halt scientific progress and bring about a return to the natural world and what he saw as a healthier primitive life. The Unabomber and his manifesto inspired discussion among philosophers, scientists, and other thinkers about the harms of technology.

## QUOTES

"Has it ever occurred to you even as a remote possibility, that your brother might be the Unabomber?"

*—Linda Patrik, to David Kaczynski*

"Ted . . . was special because he was so intelligent. In the Kaczynski family, intelligence carried high value."

*—David Kaczynski, in his book* Every Last Tie

# GLOSSARY

**affidavit**
A sworn statement in writing used to support a court proceeding, such as a request for a search warrant.

**boundary functions**
A set of advanced mathematical problems, theories, and equations.

**cipher**
A code or disguised way of writing.

**detonator**
A device that sets off an explosive charge.

**doctorate**
The highest academic degree, also known as doctor of philosophy or PhD.

**forensics**
Characterized by the use of scientific techniques to investigate a crime.

**manifesto**
A document explaining the philosophy of a group or individual.

**perpetrator**
Someone who commits a crime.

**pipe bomb**
An explosive device in which the charge is contained within a length of pipe.

## profile

A detailed description of unknown criminal suspects based on their past behavior.

## schizophrenia

A mental illness in which a person experiences delusions, hallucinations, and disordered thinking.

## sentencing

The part of a criminal trial that determines the punishment of a guilty defendant.

## stakeout

A police operation in which investigators watch a home or other location and the activities of a criminal suspect.

## stethoscope

A medical device used to listen to very faint sounds, such as a heartbeat.

## suspect

A person thought to have committed a crime.

## thesis

An academic paper that describes and attempts to prove a proposition or hypothesis.

## warrant

A court document allowing law enforcement to carry out an arrest or a search.

# ADDITIONAL RESOURCES

## SELECTED BIBLIOGRAPHY


Chase, Alston. *Harvard and the Unabomber: The Education of an American Terrorist.* W. W. Norton, 2003.

Gehring, Jamie. *Madman in the Woods: Life Next Door to the Unabomber.* Diversion Books, 2022.

Kaczynski, David. *Every Last Tie: The Story of the Unabomber and His Family.* Duke University Press, 2016.


## FURTHER READINGS


Cooper, Chris. *Forensic Science.* DK, 2020.

Denson, Bryan. *The Unabomber: Agent Kathy Puckett and the Hunt for a Serial Bomber.* Roaring Brook Press, 2019.

Morris, Rebecca. *The Olympic Park Bombing.* Abdo, 2024.


## ONLINE RESOURCES

To learn more about the Unabomber, please visit **abdobooklinks.com** or scan this QR code. These links are routinely monitored and updated to provide the most current information available.

# MORE INFORMATION

For more information on this subject, contact or visit the following organizations:

## FBI HEADQUARTERS

935 Pennsylvania Ave. NW

Washington, DC 20535

fbi.gov/contact-us/fbi-headquarters/the-fbi-experience

The FBI headquarters offers an exhibit with a self-guided tour through FBI history, allowing visitors to see artifacts from the most important criminal cases of the past. The FBI Experience includes a reconstruction of the Unabomber's cabin and fragments from one of Ted Kaczynski's homemade bombs.

## LINCOLN LIBRARY

102 Ninth Ave.

Lincoln, MT 59639

lclibrary.org/145/Lincoln

In this small community library, Ted Kaczynski spent long hours reading science magazines and studying directories of business leaders and university professors, seeking out targets for his deadly explosive packages.

## UNIVERSITY OF MICHIGAN SPECIAL COLLECTIONS RESEARCH CENTER

Harlan Hatcher Graduate Library (South)

913 S. University Ave.

Ann Arbor, MI 48109

findingaids.lib.umich.edu/catalog/umich-scl-kaczynski

The University of Michigan Special Collections Research Center is home to the Ted Kaczynski Papers, a collection of materials that Kaczynski donated to the library in 1999. The materials include letters, essays, and legal documents.

# SOURCE NOTES

## CHAPTER 1. JUST ANOTHER DAY

1. William Finnegan. "When the Unabomber Was Arrested, One of the Longest Manhunts in FBI History Was Finally Over." *Smithsonian Magazine*, May 2018, smithsonianmag.com. Accessed 3 July 2023.

2. "History: The Unabomber." *FBI*, n.d., fbi.gov. Accessed 3 July 2023.

3. "News: The Unabomber Case." *FBI*, n.d., fbi.gov. Accessed 3 July 2023.

## CHAPTER 2. DROPPING OUT

1. David Kaczynski. *Every Last Tie: The Story of the Unabomber and His Family.* Duke University Press, 2016. 2.

2. James W. Clarke. *Defining Danger: American Assassins and the New Domestic Terrorists.* Transaction Publishers, 2012. 315.

3. Jonathan Moreno. "Harvard's Experiment on the Unabomber, Class of '62." *Psychology Today*, 25 May 2012, psychologytoday.com. Accessed 3 July 2023.

4. Leigh Remizowski. "Unabomber Lists Life Sentences as Achievement." *CNN*, 24 May 2012, cnn.com. Accessed 3 July 2023.

## CHAPTER 3. SEARCHING FOR WILDERNESS

1. Jamie Gehring. *Madman in the Woods: Life Next Door to the Unabomber.* Diversion Books, 2022. 24.

2. "'Bull Manure': Report Details Unabomber's Prison Letters." *CBS News*, 25 Jan. 2016, cbsnews.com. Accessed 3 July 2023.

3. Doug Hill. "The Unabomber's Favorite Philosopher (and Mine)." *Cyborgology*, 8 June 2012, thesocietypages.org. Accessed 3 July 2023.

4. Gehring, *Madman in the Woods*, 28.

5. Serge Kovaleski. "Kaczynski Letters Reveal Tormented Mind." *Washington Post*, 20 Jan. 1997, washingtonpost.com. Accessed 3 July 2023.

## CHAPTER 4. REJECTION AND RAGE

1. Alston Chase. *Harvard and the Unabomber: The Education of an American Terrorist*. W. W. Norton, 2003. 108.

2. Stephen J. Lynton. "Bomb Jolts Jet." *Washington Post*, 16 Nov. 1979, washingtonpost.com. Accessed 3 July 2023.

## CHAPTER 5. THE MOUNTING TOLL

1. "A Chronology of the UNABOM Investigation." *Cornell*, n.d., law.cornell.edu. Accessed 3 July 2023.

2. "Excerpts from Kaczynski's Journal." *New York Times Archive*, 11 Nov. 1997, archive.nytimes.com. Accessed 3 July 2023.

3. Andrew Lenoir. "Ted Kaczynski: How a Child Math Prodigy Became the Serial-Killing Unabomber." *All That's Interesting*, 21 Sept. 2021, allthatsinteresting.com. Accessed 3 July 2023.

## CHAPTER 6. A FRUITLESS SEARCH

1. Jim Freeman, Terry D. Turchie, and Donald Max Noel. *Unabomber: How the FBI Broke Its Own Rules to Capture the Terrorist Ted Kaczynski*. History Publishing, 2014. 157.

2. Dana Getz. "The Unabomber Sketch Artist Is Famous in Her Own Right." *Bustle*, 22 Aug. 2017, bustle.com. Accessed 3 July 2023.

3. Freeman, Turchie, and Noel, *Unabomber*, 180.

## CHAPTER 7. THE MANIFESTO

1. "The Communiques of Freedom Club." *Anarchist Library*, n.d., theanarchistlibrary.org. Accessed 3 July 2023.

2. "Industrial Society and Its Future." *Washington Post*, 1995, washingtonpost.com. Accessed 3 July 2023.

3. "Industrial Society and Its Future."

4. "Industrial Society and Its Future."

5. "Unabomber Auction Nets $190,000." *NBC News*, 2 June 2011, nbcnews.com. Accessed 3 July 2023.

6 David Kaczynski. *Every Last Tie: The Story of the Unabomber and His Family*. Duke University Press, 2016. x.

7. Kaczynski, *Every Last Tie*, x.

## CHAPTER 8. LYING IN WAIT

1. David Kaczynski. *Every Last Tie: The Story of the Unabomber and His Family.* Duke University Press, 2016. 94.

2. Alston Chase. *Harvard and the Unabomber: The Education of an American Terrorist.* W. W. Norton, 2003. 111.

3. David Kaczynski, *Every Last Tie*, 99.

4. "How the FBI Caught the Unabomber." *Crime Report*, 14 June 2021, thecrimereport.org. Accessed 3 July 2023.

5. "Turchie Affidavit." *Ted K Archive*, n.d., thetedkarchive.com. Accessed 3 July 2023.

6. "Turchie Affidavit."

7. "Turchie Affidavit."

8. Chase, *Harvard and the Unabomber*, 112.

9. "News: The Unabomber Case." *FBI*, n.d., fbi.gov. Accessed 3 July 2023.

10. "Turchie Affidavit."

## CHAPTER 9. ON TRIAL

1. "20 Years Later, Montana Town Recalls Unabomber, Media Frenzy." *San Diego Union-Tribune*, 4 Apr. 2016, sandiegouniontribune.com. Accessed 3 July 2023.

2. "Who Was the Unabomber? The Real Story of What Ted Kaczynski Kept in His Cabin." *Newsweek*, 31 July 2017, newsweek.com. Accessed 3 July 2023.

3. "On the Internet, the Unabomber Is a Star." *New York Times*, 6 Apr. 1996, nytimes.com. Accessed 3 July 2023.

4. "The Unabomber Case." *Unabomber Trial*, n.d., unabombertrial.com. Accessed 3 July 2023.

5. Anneta Konstantinides. "The Pen Pal Teacher Nicknamed Lady Love Who Stole the Heart of the Unabomber." *Daily Mail*, 10 June 2023, dailymail.co.uk. Accessed 3 July 2023.

6. Brett A. Barnett. "20 Years Later: A Look Back at the Unabomber Manifesto." *Perspectives on Terrorism*, Dec. 2015, universiteitleiden.nl. Accessed 3 July 2023.

7. Thomas Kaplan. "Unabomber's Act Still Affects Prof. Gelernter." *Yale Daily News*, 1 Jan. 2009, yaledailynews.com. Accessed 3 July 2023.

8. Aaron Homer. "The Italian Unabomber Copycat That Has Never Been Caught." *Grunge*, 11 Nov. 2022, grunge.com. Accessed 3 July 2023.

# ABOUT THE AUTHOR

## TOM STREISSGUTH

Tom Streissguth is the author of more than 150 books of history, biography, and media studies for young people. He is a graduate of Yale University, where he majored in music, and has worked as a teacher and book editor. His website *The Archive of American Journalism,* which collects nonfiction articles from more than a dozen renowned American writers, has become an important resource for students and authors.